Sister Paula Vandegaer

A Life and Legacy of Service Protecting the Unborn

The Society for Sister Paula

The authors have made every effort to ensure the accuracy of the information within this book was correct at time of publication. The authors do not assume and hereby disclaim any liability to any party for any loss, damage, or disruption caused by errors or omissions, whether such errors or omissions result from accident, negligence, or any other cause.

Mentoris Project
745 South Sierra Madre Drive
San Marino, CA 91108

Copyright © 2022 The Society for Sister Paula

More information at www.sisterpaulasociety.org

ISBN: 978-1-947431-52-2

"It was all based on sound, scientific counseling principles: acceptance, nonjudgmental attitude, individuation, listening, and confidentiality."

"Most young women choose abortions out of fear, not out of desire. When we deal with the fear, they universally choose life."

—*Sister Paula Vandegaer*

Introduction

Through the influence of Sister Paula Vandegaer, we all are encouraged to participate in the pro-life movement. She led us into unaccustomed activities such as fundraising, debating, and encouraging other followers. And as followers ourselves, we were motivated not to accept failure but accept the challenge to look forward to alternatives to ensure the movement succeed. Failure was never accepted in working with Sister Paula, and we were met with camaraderie with like-minded people.

The issue surrounding the pro-life movement has caused a reawakening of our purpose, with fundamental questions: Is there a Creator? Is there a purpose? Is there an obligation to preserve life? These issues are a test to the connection with our humanity. We have seen infanticide through ethnic discrimination, race intolerance, gender preference, and the cleansing of challenging birth defects, by massive abortions on demand.

As long as Sister Paula was around, we had a lively connection to these questions. She was our leader and defended our beliefs. Now that she is no longer with us, are we lost?

Unequivocally no.

It turns out we have someone looking over us. Her passing created a focus on the living issues for saving lives. It is an axiom that through death there is new life. To that end, the Society for Sister Paula was established to recognize and continue in spirit what she did in life.

It is our aim to recognize Sister Paula as a poster person for the pro-life movement. We want to recognize her and promote the life-sustaining issues that she stood for. It is our mission that by whatever means possible to attest to her life and devotion by praying for her intercession in caring for the weakest members of society.

Through the passage of time, her grace will permeate the hearts and minds of people who are confronted with life and death issues. In our mission for the Society for Sister Paula, we are not focused on the legal aspects but simply to win hearts and minds through faith and reason. We are unabashed in protecting life, from the womb to the end of life.

—The Society for Sister Paula

The Call to Service

In 1939, Kansas City, Missouri, marked the end of an era and the beginning of a new one. The mayor of this midwestern city was convicted of not paying taxes and was sentenced to fifteen months in jail, after years of corruption involving bribery, gambling and prostitution.

Into this world of corruption, a small devout Kansas City family celebrated the birth of a daughter whose God-filled life was to change the world for the better.

Thomas Vandegaer, a working man originally from Louisiana, was a telegraph operator for the Kansas City Railroad. His wife, Lillian, was born and raised in Kansas City.

Their daughter, named Elsie Ann, heard God's call to her at a young age, when she was just a teenager. At age seventeen she joined the Sisters of

Social Service in Kansas City. In a black-and-white photo from that time she stares at the camera with a warm smile—she appears to be a slim, dark-eyed young woman with an innocent face, wearing a nun's habit. After taking her vows and completing her training, this young woman eventually took the name of Paula.

Her parents must have worried when their daughter left her Midwestern home for college in California.

A bright, intelligent young woman, Sister Paula attended Immaculate Heart College, a private college located in Los Angeles, which offered religious education as well as courses in art. It must have been eye-opening to Sister Paula, a Kansas City girl, to see the mountains and rugged western landscapes, to wonder at the year-round fine weather—and to study alongside so many other young students like herself. She graduated in 1963 with a bachelor's degree in psychology.

Inspired by her education, she went on to get a master's degree in social work two years later from the Catholic University of America, another private school, this one located in Washington, D.C. This was the 1960s in America and social behaviors were changing. Sister Paula remembered it this way:

"I was studying at Catholic University during the 60s and on my way to becoming a professional social worker. It was an exciting decade. The second Vatican Council opened October 1962 and things began changing. The intellectual setting I was in was a hotbed for new ideas. It seemed every day we heard about new formulations in theology and new regulations from the Church. The Liturgy changed dramatically, and everyone was alert to the 'new.'"

One controversial cultural turning point was new access to the birth control pill, which was becoming widely popular and known simply as "the Pill." Sister Paula grappled with its implication as a contraceptive, and eventually concluded that she could never recommend it to women. Not only could "the Pill" lead to marital infidelity, it could also be used to induce early abortion.

Sister Paula returned to Los Angeles after receiving her graduate degree and obtaining her license as a clinical social worker. Here she began working as a psychotherapist, work that required her to listen—intuitively and with no judgement—to clients. Doing so gave clients space to freely share their deepest fears, worries, dark secrets, and most fervent wishes.

Because Sister Paula had such an aptitude for

this kind of work, one has to assume that she had these qualities even before her training began.

"She had a kind of charisma," said Sister Shaun Marie Wise who knew Sister Paula in her early years in Los Angeles. "She was able to reach out to other people."

When Sister Paula returned to Los Angeles at the age of twenty-six in 1965 she started working with the Catholic Youth Organization and then at the Holy Family Adoption Agency, located in on South Westlake Avenue in downtown Los Angeles. She and other Sisters were assigned to counsel women and men at this facility. It was a three-story building a few blocks from St. Vincent Hospital, and clients could make an appointment for counseling or drop in.

Sister Shaun Marie worked with Sister Paula at the Holy Family. "There were three of us in what they called the Natural Parent Unit," she explained. Other units included the adoption services and foster services. Working side-by-side, the three Sisters bonded and enjoyed each other's company. They became lasting friends.

"She did have a very spirited personality," recalled Sister Shaun Marie who now lives at the Sisters of Social Service Center in Encino,

California. "We took women from any background and any faith and helped them work out what they wanted to do. Abortion was still illegal in California. There was also a foster care unit, and an adoption unit there, and another agency nearby called St. Anne's Home run by Franciscan sisters. If we had a girl who didn't have a place to go or anyone to help her, she could go there. A lot of these women had terrible financial struggles."

This focus on pregnant women in trouble captured Sister Paula's interest at a deep level. Here were people left in a crisis to defend for themselves.

"Holy Family is where she first got interested in and involved with life issues," said Sister Patricia McGowen who also knew her at the time. "That was where she really became acutely aware the issues of an unwanted pregnancy being terminated. Away she went! She was a one-person operation."

Sister Paula witnessed the struggles faced by unwed pregnant women and girls, including being abandoned by their boyfriends and families with nowhere to turn for help, circumstances that could push them to seek an illegal abortion. Stepping in to help was exactly the kind of work that Sisters of Social Service, including Sister Paula, had vowed to do.

She had found her true calling—work that combined her spiritual belief in the sanctity of human life and utilized her skills as a social worker.

The Sisters of Social Service order was established in 1923 in Hungary by Sister Margaret Slachta, who was also a member of that country's Parliament. She advocated for the well-being of women, children and families. These sisters dedicated themselves to responding to the needs of people who were disadvantaged socially and economically—and this usually meant women and children. Their numbers grew as the Sisters of Social Service also became established in Slovakia, Romania, Canada, China, and the United States. The Sisters wore gray dresses and worked directly with people in need.

The Sisters' work sometimes put them in grave danger—particularly when Sister Sara Salkahazi and Sister Margaret Slachta, tried to save Jewish refugees by creating safe houses for those fleeing for their lives during the holocaust.

When Sister Paula entered the order at the young age of seventeen, she knew that the work ahead would put her in direct contact with people suffering with seemingly insurmountable problems—and that doing God's work could sometimes be dangerous.

She certainly learned that the Sisters of Social Service in Europe had saved lives—something she herself would eventually do.

By all accounts, she embraced this work with energy, intelligence and always a profound sense of hope.

In her early years of counseling women at Holy Family Adoption Agency, Sister Paula's optimism was evident, and sometimes contagious. "She was fun!" recalled Sister Shaun Marie with a laugh. "One time the agency had a fundraiser and Sister Paula said that we three [Sisters] should sing—and we did! She really did exude life and spirit."

Lighthearted as she was, Sister Paula was serious about protecting mothers and their unborn babies.

One incident served as her awakening: While working at Holy Family Adoption Agency, Sister Paula met a young woman who'd been pressured to have an abortion and told to reject the possibility of adoption. "The welfare worker told her that abortion was new and safe and legal, and that 'it' was only tissue in the early stages," said Sister Paula later recalling what the young woman had told her. The young pregnant woman was made to feel that she was foolish for even considering another alternative. "We had quite a long discussion, and she decided there was nothing wrong with her if she placed her baby for adoption. I was absolutely furious," she said. "I realized that something had to be done to protect these women."

Being a leader, an organizer, and an activist were probably not in Sister Paula's expectations for her future. But following the call of God can sometimes take people into new worlds and responsibilities, if they can hear that call and have the courage to do what is asked. This is exactly what happened to Sister Paula in the next decades of her life.

Reaching Pregnant Women in Crisis

"On June 14, 1967, Ronald Reagan signed the Therapeutic Abortion Act, after only six months as California governor. From a total of 518 legal abortions in California in 1967, the number of abortions would soar to an annual average of 100,000 in the remaining years of Reagan's two terms—more abortions than in any U.S. state prior to the advent of Roe v. Wade. Reagan's signing of the abortion bill was an ironic beginning for a man often seen as the modern father of the pro-life movement."

—*National Review*

The late 1960s and early 1970s were years of upheaval. America was roiled by protests against the Vietnam War, and by women and Black citizens demanding equal pay and opportunities.

But another powerful movement was afoot that was much quieter but no less powerful—the pro-life movement.

In 1967 Colorado was the first state in the country to loosen restrictions on abortion, followed by North Carolina and California. (Reagan said later his liberalized abortion bill had led to "abortion on demand" in California and that he wouldn't make that mistake again.)

Sister Paula's energy shifted into high gear. At the young age of twenty-eight, she was ready do whatever she could to save the lives of the unborn.

How could she protect pregnant women and their babies? She was not the only person asking this question.

Ronald Reagan was governor of California from 1967 to 1975. When he signaled that he might decide to relax some restrictions for abortion early in his first term, pro-life advocates in California began to come together. This was the beginning of what was to become the "Right to Life" movement, explained Margaret ("Peggy") Hartshorn, PhD, in her book, *Foot Soldiers Armed with Love*. "A loose coalition of pro-life people of various professions got together to fight this legislation and to lobby against the bill in the California legislature, and they eventually called themselves the Right to Life League (believed to be the first pro-life group to organize in the United States and use the name 'right to life,' and one of the first to offer pregnancy help services)."

This group was in contact with a member of the Sisters of Social Service who urged Sister Paula to get involved, Hartshorn noted.

No convincing was needed—Sister Paula was already all-in. She was so dedicated to this cause that when the Right to Life League was incorporated in 1969, Sister Paula was named a board member.

But she had a unique perspective on the problem and the solution. Because of her social work training, she recognized that pregnant women in the middle of a crushing and yet private dilemma did not need scolding or recrimination but rather support and compassion to make this critical choice about what to do. They needed a safe place to think, to understand the full implications of their choice, and a kind ear to listen to them.

How could she reach these women so that they would not automatically choose abortion?

"In those years pro-life people were struggling to learn how to educate people on the dangers of abortion to women and family life and to explain that there is a live human baby in utero," Sister Paula wrote in her book, *Introduction to Pregnancy Counseling*—a manual that is still used to this day.

> "From the beginning counselors realized that many women who choose abortion do so believing that it is a simple solution to a complex problem. Some believe that there is not really a baby in the womb and that there will be few negative consequences following this decision. In fact, this is not the case."

The idea of a pregnancy counseling center, a private place where women could discretely get the help they needed in their time of crisis, was an immediate solution to many pro-life activists. The first one was established in Toronto in 1968, and, according to Sister Paula, by 1972 there were sixty such centers in the United States. Today there are thousands.

Some called this type of crisis counseling

developed by Sister Paula and learned by hundreds of others, the "pregnancy help movement."

But how to reach women who could not find their way to one of these centers and who were alone and unprepared to make a decision about their pregnancy? A pro-life pregnancy hotline was established in 1971 in Whittier, California, by another passionate pro-life woman—Margaret Nemecek—who founded what is now called Whittier Life Center.

Hotlines were rare at that time. It was a huge innovation to have calls routed to the homes of volunteers. These calls came from all over the country. Sister Paula agreed to train the volunteers to answer the phones—most of these were Nemecek's neighbors, relatives, friends and mothers of her children's playmates, remembers her daughter Corie Austin, who herself was trained by Sister Paula.

"Sister Paula was very soft spoken, she had a nice beautiful voice and she would listen a lot," said Austin. "She'd ask, 'What did you think of that? or 'Why did you do that?' We would try to help the women make a decision they could live with the rest of their lives."

Margaret Nemecek was so devoted to the pro-life work that Sister Paula decided to present her with an award, but when Nemecek sensed that this was going to happen she resisted.

"It was Sister Paula's idea," said Nemecek's daughter. "What I remember is that my family and I were in the car going to Mass at St. Mary's on Whittier on a Sunday. My mother sensed something was different and she said, 'I am not going,' and wouldn't get out of the car. But somehow we got her into the pews and Sister Paula gave her an award in front of everybody."

Austin said her mother never wanted to be praised and preferred to work in the background, but Sister Paula wanted to acknowledge her—and then other people too.

Sister Paula called it the Nemecek Award and each year she presented it to someone in the pro-life movement who had done steady, dedicated work. Recipients have included Tom Glessner of the National Institute of Family and Life Advocates, Archbishop José Gomez of Los Angeles, Robert Barbera, and many others.

Corie Austin continues to answer hotline calls—some that come in the middle of the night. She never judges but offers a kind ear and encouragement to call again, stay in touch. One such young woman who decided to have her baby was so grateful that she named her baby Corie.

Crisis intervention for women experiencing an unexpected pregnancy was a new field. "It was our movement that really developed this new area of counseling," Sister Paula was reported to have stated.

Establishing a counseling center was a complicated process—there were real estate, legal and logistical issues—but the most desperate need was training for the volunteers who wanted to work at the centers. How to transmit Sister Paula's practical wisdom to large groups of volunteers?

Sister Paula, drawing from her education, experience and therapeutic skills, put down all she knew in *Introduction to Pregnancy Counseling*, which detailed guidance toward understanding the extreme and difficult circumstances for many pregnant women, and how to listen and respond to them while providing compassionate counselling. This was the first book of its kind.

Here are a few insights from Sister Paula that reveal her training as a social worker, and her depth of understanding in how to approach women:

"Pro-life counseling is based on the belief that people do not come to us to be lectured, but to sort out their feelings and to be given the truth. When people understand the truth, they can then make an informed decision."

"Closely allied to listening is acceptance. Jane has probably already talked to someone and may have already gotten some judgmental feedback. *You mean you got yourself pregnant? How could you have done such a stupid thing?* The strongest thing that you have going for you is your attitude of acceptance. You are not going to get upset with her for what she did. Remember, this is a young woman who has a lot of feelings that are already making her feel very uncomfortable about herself as a person."

"When we first start in pro-life counseling, it may be difficult to be nonjudgmental when the woman is talking about an abortion. We must remember she would not be requesting an abortion if she felt it were morally wrong. She is requesting an abortion because of problems in her life that make her feel that bringing a pregnancy to term is too much for her now and she feels that she cannot respond to a baby in her future."

"Our listening, acceptance, and nonjudgmental attitude will help her gain inner strength and gain control of her feelings. This will help her to feel able to take care of the child growing within her and thus be more willing to have her baby."

Sister Paula's book explores the reasons why a young pregnant woman may want an abortion and explains exactly how to understand her, talk to her, educate her and offer guidance in her decision.

Years later, Sister Paula talked about her approach, which was aligned with that of the Catholic Church: "While law and society often pit the interests of a mother against those of her unborn child, the Church recognizes that their best interests are joined. What is best for the child is also best for the mother."

In her personality and demeanor, Sister Paula

epitomized the quality of compassion of a true counselor. Every person who met her was struck by her calm nature, her steady voice and easy smile. And she was trustworthy.

Peggy Hartshorn wrote: "Sister Paula always emphasized the importance of listening carefully to each woman's story and treating her in a loving, caring, and non-judgmental way, the importance of discovering who she is, affirming her, and helping her discern the best choice for her baby and herself, based on who God created her to be as a woman (as Sister might say, the 'psychology' of who she is as a woman and the difference between what abortion and motherhood will mean to her as a woman.)"

Sister Paula's manual continues to guide pregnancy counselors. "Bits of almost every pregnancy help training program today can be traced to her first pregnancy counseling manual from 1971, developed for the first ever pregnancy help hotline," wrote Peggy Hartshorn.

Putting the woman at the center of the discussion—and supporting this mother in her crisis—might enable her to feel cared for and safe enough to give birth to her baby.

Ann Vaughn volunteered to answer hotline

calls when she herself was a young mother. "We were told not to judge but just to help with any or all resources a woman might need," she remembers. Calls to the hotline were routed to her home phone line so she could volunteer easily a few hours each week.

"I was given a resource book that was about four or five inches thick, full of resources," she said, "including licensed counselors who would come to your home to talk to your parents about your pregnancy if you were afraid to tell them. We had resources for how to sign up for free medical care, and if you needed help after the baby was born, how to get cribs, strollers and other items through a nearby center."

One resource really stood out to her: "The most striking was that if a woman got kicked out of her house because she was pregnant there were a list of people who would take in a pregnant woman to live in their homes for free during the pregnancy."

But Vaughn remembers that mostly her role was to listen to the callers. "They really needed to talk to somebody," she said. "They were by themselves and their heads were spinning with fear. They were listening to everyone around them saying this is going to ruin their life. If they could just stop and just get really quiet in themselves listen to what they want to do, they would choose to keep the baby—if they had help. None of them wanted to go have an abortion. They were feeling pressured and didn't feel they had anywhere to go. They were really alone and really scared, so we would get them out of fear, and say, 'Here's the help we can offer you. Just having a friendly person to talk to was important."

Vaughn was given lengthy training for this volunteer job that included watching videos made by Sister Paula, and found the work extremely satisfying. "For me it was a good volunteer opportunity," she said.

How many babies were born due to Sister Paula's compassion and that of her many volunteers? Sister Paula was never interested in keeping these kinds of statistics—instead she wanted the care of individual women and their babies to be at the center of pro-life discussions. She wanted most of all to build healthy, happy families in which babies could thrive.

In the early 1970s more pregnancy counseling centers were opening, and Sister Paula sought ways to bring directors and counselors together so that she could widely communicate her professional expertise in how to counsel women.

Holding conferences was an effective way for center directors and volunteer counselors to get to know each other and share their best practices. The first conference took place in 1971 on a college campus in Minnesota, according to the historical timeline of Heartbeat International. Every year, these conferences grew in attendance, and most were held in California where Sister Paula was living.

"These were thee-day conferences usually held in Southern California once a year," recalled Nancy Corbett, who worked for many years as the Executive Director of the Mission Hills, California Pregnancy Counseling Center. "Sister Paula got great speakers. We learned fundraising ideas, how to handle difficult clients, and how to counsel women who'd had an abortion who might be stuffing down their feelings. Sister Paula was so good at this. She was a very intelligent woman."

Her reputation for bringing famous speakers was well known, and later, when Sister Paula created the Advanced Training Institute as part of International Life Services, the speakers she brought to make presentations were influential pro-life figures.

"They were international speakers," recalled Donna Sorek, who was trained by Sister Paula and worked in the Ventura County pregnancy help center in Ventura, California.

Vicki Thorn, Director of the National Office of Post-Abortion Reconciliation and Healing and founder of Project Rachel was one speaker Sorek remembered. Abby Johnson, former worker at Planned Parenthood, was another. Sister Paula also brought in Greg Lester, a psychologist, educator and a leading author. "She met him because she herself was really well-known as a leader in counseling," said Sorek.

All the volunteers, including Sorek, soaked up the wisdom from these leaders. "We needed to know how to counsel those women," she said.

Sister Paula insisted that volunteers receive a high level of training in counseling, and Sorek was deeply moved by this. Volunteers were not left to figure this out on the own. "Sister Paula was remarkable in the quality of the training she gave," Sorek said. "That was a big part of her contribution—she insisted that when you come in to volunteer, you end up receiving a caliber of training on the level of a professional therapist. She was a social worker and she followed latest research. She really wanted us to do this as a kind of continuing education. She always insisted that the backbone of pro-life work had to be pro-life counseling."

Sorek was also struck by Sister Paula's commitment to do what she knew in her heart was right. "One thing that stands out about Sister Paula is that she was always true to her principles," said Sorek. "She instilled in me that every client needed to be listened to, every client was an individual. They weren't statistics."

With help from Robert Barbera, Sister Paula made videos of her counseling trainings. "We produced these tapes specifically for counseling," said Barbera who had connected with a marketing professional who wanted to donate to the pro-life cause and funded the project. This man found a studio in Orange County in Southern California where Sister Paula could record her trainings on how to counsel women. "She did a beautiful job," recalled Barbera. The tapes were later transferred to CDs which were distributed to counselors at pregnancy counseling centers around the country.

Making training videotapes, organizing conventions, coordinating trainings for hundreds of volunteers—Sister Paula was now working on a larger scale. And like a missionary she plunged into unknown territory to do the work of God. Her courageous spirit led her to develop these new skills, skills she never knew she had. And this also included writing and speaking to large groups. It was as if she lived by this philosophy: If it had to be done to advance the cause, she would learn to do it.

In addition to these pro-life activities, Sister Paula still kept up her work as a private therapist. "It was at this time Sister Paula continued doing counselling at night for distressed people in order to supplement the overhead at the agency," recalled Barbera.

Following Sister Paula's death in August of 2021, moving testimonies about her dedication to the cause poured in. She not only affected individuals personally, but she helped secure pro-life institutions so that they could survive and thrive.

Monsignor John Moretta, who served with Sister Paula on the board of the Right to Life League in the 1980s shared a revealing memory. When he and his parishioners decided to open a pregnancy help center in East Los Angeles, he contacted Sister Paula for guidance—and she knew exactly what needed to be done.

"Sister Paula handled the insurance, the

legalities, and even staffed the center," he said. In other words, she made sure it happened. This pregnancy center in East Los Angeles still operates today.

Once again Sister Paula had learned how to dive into the details of what was needed for the survival of pregnancy centers, and she did it.

But Sister Paula's work—and that of the entire pro-life movement—was soon to become much more challenging. It was time for allies in the movement to pool their energy and resources to work together.

Joining Forces

THE YEAR 1971 WAS A TURNING POINT FOR SISTER Paula and others in the growing pro-life movement. The pregnancy help center in Whittier, California, began providing pregnancy tests—this way pregnant women could receive counseling immediately after learning their results. And in this year, Sister Paula met two people who were already pro-life powerhouses: Dr. John Hillabrand and Mrs. Lore Maier.

Dr. Hillabrand was a Catholic and an obstetrician/gynecologist who began his practice in Toledo, Ohio, in 1938 and went on to deliver thousands of babies. He believed that life began at conception and that it must be protected from that moment. He cared about mothers and babies equally and was dedicated to the pro-life movement. He began the Toledo pregnancy center with the help of his nurse, Esther Applegate.

Mrs. Lore Maier was born in Germany in 1923 and had lost many family members during World War II. After the war, she performed humanitarian work and in 1951 she came to United States and married. Her traumatic experiences in Germany formed her deep passion for life and her desire to protect it. She and her husband moved to Toledo and Mrs. Maier became an inspirational pro-life speaker in the U.S.

At a meeting in Toronto in 1971, Dr. Hillabrand, Mrs. Maier, and Sister Paula Vandegaer came to the realization that a national organization for the pregnancy help centers was needed so that they could all operate more effectively. The three founders called this organization Alternatives to Abortion Incorporated—or AAI—which was later renamed Heartbeat International. Although all three founders were Catholic, they had no intention of creating an organization that was solely Catholic—they preferred their work to be known as humanitarian.

An immediate priority was to coordinate contact information for all the pregnancy help centers in the United States—there were about 100 in 1972—so that information could be shared easily among them. This was the first time all the centers were unified, and this made them stronger.

Sister Paula worked closely with Lore Maier, who wrote a manual called *Suggested Guidelines for Establishing Pro-Life Emergency Pregnancy Service Centers*.

Hartshorn quoted Sister Paula when she recalled those first years: "It was so exciting to see all the energy—the Holy Spirit was moving throughout the land, and all before 1973! Once we had the manuals, from then on it went like crazy—centers were starting at a rate of two per week! The movement was so rapid, so incredible. I was traveling all over to give trainings from New York to Hawaii. Our feeling was, for God's sake, get them going."

It was a devastating blow to the burgeoning pro-life movement when the Supreme Court legalized abortion in 1973 with the Roe vs. Wade case. Yet Sister Paula and many others responded by increasing their efforts to open more pregnancy counseling centers—some supported by Catholic organizations, others by ecumenical groups. Sister Paula recalled that pivotal moment. "People were just pouring out of the woodwork to do something about what the Supreme Court had done."

She knew that by disseminating information she could keep all the centers connected and informed. In 1977, Sister Paula helped produce a magazine for AAI called *Heartbeat*. Had she ever created a magazine before in her life? Of course not, but this did not stop her. If it would help reach more women, inspire counselors in aiding women to choose life rather than abortion, then she would find a way to create a publication to be distributed and read widely.

Funding came from individual donations that seemingly arrived out of the blue, and from small fundraisers. Sister Paula just barely brought in enough money to print the magazine.

At this time, she met Kathy Hochderffer, an artist who provided the magazine's first sketch—the image of a pregnant woman leaning against a tree. The image came from a dream that Kathy had and she told Sister Paula about it. The woman represented a friend of Kathy's who'd killed herself after having an abortion. The scene also includes light shining down through the forest onto the woman—the light of God and hope.

Sister Paula was entranced by the image, and how perfectly it represented Christ and the Church shining light in the darkest places in the human heart.

Heartbeat magazine was an ideal outlet for Sister Paula to write about all aspects of the pro-life issue. She edited and published this magazine as well as other publications. Through them she articulated many dimensions of pro-life beliefs—and these writings inspired readers for years to come, and even after her death.

Two articles—"Helping a Sexually Active Woman to Say No" and "The Guidance of the Spirit in Our Counseling"—had a major impact on Peggy Hartshorn.

"I used to take these two articles into the room with me while I waited for the results of the client's pregnancy test (this was before centers began 'self-testing' and before we had medical clinics), and I read them over and over to give me insight and courage before I went out again to talk to the client," wrote Hartshorn in her book, *Foot Soldiers Armed with Love*.

Sister Paula believed that whether or not a client learned that she was pregnant from these test results she might benefit from considering her sexuality in the context of dignity and self respect—a potentially life-changing perspective.

And all the while, more and more pregnancy counseling centers were quietly opening across the country. In 1977, AAI knew there were at least 782 of them in the U.S.

More pregnant women were receiving compassionate help than ever before and choosing not to abort.

Think of the Baby

A core message of Sister Paula's pro-life counseling was to urge pregnant women to think of the baby. A member of the Right to Life League of Southern California remembered being coached by Sister Paula when she began to do crisis pregnancy counseling on the phone and wrote about this on an online legacy page after Sister Paula's death. "I always remembered that she told me that the most important thing was to get the client 'to think of the baby,'" wrote the volunteer.

Part of this care included helping women get jobs so that they could care for their babies. Sister Paula secured help from a Southern California bank and a grocery store chain whose CEOs were willing to train the women.

Donna Sorek remembered one dramatic story that shows just how critical this training could be.

"It was one of my first few suicide calls. She had every reason to be upset. She was twenty-three, pregnant, her family had walked out on her, her boyfriend had left her, and she had no education." Sorek counseled the young woman, who decided to have her baby. Afterward, Sorek was able to connect her with an entry-level job at a bank. "She entered as a teller, and worked her way up," Sorek recalled. "When her son was about ten or eleven we started to get checks in the mail—they were from this woman. She said we helped her at a time when she needed it and she was doing well, and her son was doing well. Later I was invited her son's high school graduation. She worked herself up to management position in the bank and raised her son as a single mom."

But most of the time, volunteers never knew what decision their clients chose to make. If they did have the baby, many help centers were able to give items to new mothers. "We were connected to a place called Mary's Closet, which had clothing for the child clear up to age seven," said Sorek. "We could provide baby food, formula, baby shampoo. We would give the mother a baby shower and each woman got a layette. For a while we also offered parenting classes, which was particularly important for the teen moms."

At Sorek's center one winter, a woman donated a bundle of children's clothing, saying the center had helped her years before when she was deciding whether or not to go through with her pregnancy. On Christmas Eve, a thirteen-year-old boy knocked on the door. When a volunteer opened the door, he said "My mom told me I should come and tell you, I am that baby."

Donna Sorek was deeply influenced by Sister Paula's insistence on seeing every person as unique and worthy of care and compassion.

"Sister Paula really emphasized that this is a person and that we never want to lose sight of that. Each mom, each baby. Even in post-abortive situations, dads can be hurting and need to talk. She always said, we're here for the client. She made it so human."

In her pregnancy counseling book, Sister Paula's sensitivity to the pregnant client is evident. "Always get [a woman's] permission to give her information about fetal growth and development," she wrote. "'Would you like to know what your baby looks like now? Would you like to see a picture of your baby at this stage?' There are numerous publications and pamphlets available which show the beauty of fetal development in utero. Show them to her and give her some literature if you have it. While giving her the publication, slowly read and discuss it with her to help her understand the miracle inside her."

But in order for babies to be saved, Sister Paula knew that mothers had to feel safe and cared for themselves, and she believed in supporting new mothers—particularly those who are unwed—emotionally and financially after giving birth. What did this mean exactly?

It was very practical. It meant providing access to clothing and diapers and job counseling so that they could be good mothers and "form positive families," Sister Paula said. In today's parlance, this might be called "holistic" care for the new mother and her baby.

Corie Austin said the Whittier Life Center did just this by providing donated clothing, diapers and other baby items to mothers who had no resources. But even before the birth, Austin says, she counsels pregnant women to take their prenatal vitamins and do all they can to be healthy for themselves and for the baby. "We try to help the women get on their feet," she said, adding that they sometimes refer pregnant women to Precious Life Shelter, an emergency program for pregnant women who have nowhere to live.

Sister Paula understood that a central organization was needed for the pro-life movement. By now she had emerged as an inspirational leader and effective organizer for the movement and she had a long-term perspective.

By 1980, pro-life activism had gained a strong footing and Sister Paula teamed up with Msgr. John Moretta in Los Angeles to support the new Right to Life League.

"Sister Paula was a guiding light for the pro-life movement," said Anne Hennessy, former CEO of the Right to Life League. "She was a creative thinker, an energetic activist and above everything, an inspiration to us all."

Sister Paula's death was difficult for those who knew her because she had always been so charismatic and inspirational, yet also down-to-earth and practical—an unusual and dynamic combination.

Her passing left a big hole," said Tom Glessner, who founded of the National Institute of Family and

Life Advocates (NIFLA). Glessner had approached Sister Paula in 1993 to ask her to sit on NIFLA's board of directors, which she immediately agreed to do. "She was always Sister Paula—she had no ego at all," recalled Glessner, who worked with her for decades. "She was very humble and gentle. The Lord used her mightily in her work."

She was motivated always by the desire to protect the sanctity of the life of the unborn child.

She, too, always thought of the baby.

There came a time when Sister Paula needed to create a new organization that more effectively supported her views and purpose.

Her longtime friend, Robert Barbera explained what happened. "A turf war was going between Sister Paula and a midwestern pro-life agency. Sister Paula was the editor for a pro-life magazine and not properly funded to cover the cost—she wrote most of the material for the magazine and distributed the magazine. She asked me to represent her in a meeting in Washington, D.C. to settle a dispute," he said. At this meeting, were several other pro-life agencies represented from New Zealand, Texas, and New Orleans. These groups were concerned about who was to be in charge and the direction of the pro-life movement. The budget was a big concern and how to raise the funds to carry on the various programs.

"I realized Sister Paula was raising money for her magazine and could not get help from certain other pro-life groups," said Barbera. "They were not satisfied with the magazine's content. I realized these were not friendly or sympathetic groups so on behalf of Sister Paula, I let them know we would not be associated with them."

By the time Barbera returned to Los Angeles, Sister Paula had learned how he had represented her. "She thanked me for my bluntness," he said.

It was 1985 and within months, she and her close allies, including Kathy Hochderffer, founded International Life Services. This was to be a nonprofit, non-sectarian organization with three goals: education, counseling, and bioethics.

But primarily it was to provide training and education on all aspects of the sanctity of life. Kathy Hochderffer has been quoted as saying, "A well-informed public is a strong defense for the pro-life movement." This was a quote that Sister Paula reiterated many times throughout her life, and it reflected her profound belief in education as a way to open up the eyes of the public to the sanctity of life.

Robert Barbera was named vice president, and then later became president of International Life Services. In this way he was able to assist Sister Paula do what she needed to do. "In the next few months, I purchased a printing press for Sister Paula to print newsletters and other material, which was a money saver," he explained.

"She was the editor and wrote most of the newsletter's material and organized the fundraising program by telephone solicitation," he remembered. "As president my activity at that time was to establish no less than fifteen pregnancy counseling centers, solicitation by telephone and numerous letters to cover our overhead. The success can be attributed to Sister Paula who developed a name in the pro-life community by public speaking, collecting followers' names, giving seminars, publishing a magazine, and getting volunteers to be on the board.

Years later, Sister Paula admitted to having moments of doubt about the finances.

"I accumulated bills of $635, and I didn't have any money," she recalled in a video. "And I sat in my little office and thought 'What in God's name am I doing? How did I get into this? I don't know what I'm doing. I'm not a fundraiser—I'm a social worker. I do counseling. I'm printing a magazine, I'm not a printer, I don't like to write. How did I get into this? What have you done to me, God?' Although I still had a sense that I had to do it. I sat there and thought, 'Well, I'll just open the mail.' So, I opened the mail, and that day, we got donations of $630. And you know, we had five dollars in the bank. So, I had all the money we needed to pay our bills. That was a miracle to me. I sat there and thought 'Okay, why am I asking what am I doing? I'm not doing it, *you're* doing it. You're in charge of this office so what am I worrying about? You're the Executive Director and I'm your obedient servant."

Faith and Joy

Despite her many weighty responsibilities, Sister Paula managed to keep a balance in her life and work. Among her friends, family and colleagues, she was famous for her sense of humor and readiness for adventure.

"Sister Paula, in a unique way, radiated the joy and love that animate the pro-life movement," said Daniel Mansueto, president of the board of International Life Services in a remembrance after her death.

She had another quality which Mansueto struggled to define: "Anyone who knew Sister Paula within the pro-life movement would tell you she had extreme charisma," he said. "If you read about religious leaders in the past a lot of them are talked about with reverence. But if you only read about it, you don't get it. When I met Sister

Paula, I thought, now I get it. She had tremendous charisma. It's hard to articulate what it consisted of. One component was that she was very affirming. This goes to her leadership qualities. She built people up. She always affirmed peoples' virtues and what they could contribute. She did it very naturally with sincerity."

Mansueto, who first met Sister Paula after sending an email asking how he could get involved in the pro-life cause, was pleased when she helped him find work in the movement. "There was something special about her," he recalled. "She was an extremely calm person and that was very reassuring. She was completely enveloped with the pro-life cause. She lived, ate, drank, slept breathed every moment for the pro-life cause. That was her whole life. She was a very good public speaker who had this calm reassuring presence."

Her compassion could transform people around her. "I was very angry that people would even dare killing a baby," said Mechtild Grothues, a longtime pro-life activist of the La Habra Life Center in California. She met Sister Paula around 1974 when she participated in a training course and talked about her feelings when she first got involved in the pro-life movement. "I thought a woman who does this needs God's punishment. But Sister Paula taught us to be compassionate, to have empathy for these women and that really struck me. She had so much love and empathy. She suggested that we ask more questions so we could understand the situation. This compassion from Sister Paula turned my anger into love and compassion and empathy. I learned a lot from Sister Paula."

Grothues remembered a time when she was frustrated that the Church leadership was not acknowledging certain pro-life efforts. She brought it up with Sister Paula—but Sister Paula would not engage in criticism of the Church. "She never put anyone down," said Grothues. "Instead, she said, 'Hmm let's think about this.'"

Sister Paula's charisma came through when she spoke to large groups about pro-life issues, holding her audiences spellbound. After hearing her, many people immediately signed up to volunteer.

"The first time I met Sister Paula was to hear her on the podium at the end of the mass in Holy Family Catholic Church," said Robert Barbera recalling a moment with his first wife, Bernice. "We were so mesmerized and could easily relate to her after losing a child by hemorrhaging. It was at this time Sister Paula asked for volunteers and my wife Bernice decided to volunteer. Bernice worked at the office several times before she and a friend convinced me to help." Barbera spent the next decades working with Sister Paula and helping support her pro-life efforts, which included the founding of International Life Services.

Sister Paula was a social person who exuded enthusiasm for life. She had many longtime devoted friends including Kathy Hochderffer and Sister Beth Momberg, and many other Sisters of Social Service. And though she made her home in California, Sister Paula enjoyed travelling.

She played music and read many books. Energized by her faith and a positive outlook, Sister Paula could be lighthearted even in gloomy times, lifting the spirits of all those around her.

"She was a very happy person, very content with herself," said Dennis De Pietro, who worked with Sister Paula for years and currently serves on the ILS board. "She played the piano and the guitar and sang. At her Christmas parties many of us would get together and sing songs, and there was gift giving. It was incredibly wholesome—she was a Midwest persona, it shined through her."

But he was careful to explain an important

distinction. "She wasn't like a comedian," he said, "she would exude joy. She was a joyful person. And at times we'd have a board meeting about some legislation that would have happened, and we would all be down, but she'd always keep on moving."

And she was honest and forthright—some might even say blunt. "Personally, she would say what she wanted to say," said De Pietro. "But she was always concerned about people who worked around her. She was not an aggressive task master."

Anne Hennessy had this memory: "For many years we had a personal relationship rather than just a business relation. I found that she was one of those rare people that seemed to embody the love of Christ. She was always so even-tempered, always kind—she didn't seem to have a bad bone in her body that I ever saw. Occasionally we managed to have lunch together and she always had a smile. She was kind to everybody. She treated everyone as if she saw Christ in them. Her treatment was always so respectful and kind and even loving."

Germaine Wensley laughed when she recounted an adventure she had with Sister Paula. Wensley is a nurse, and years ago, when she wanted to find out how to volunteer for the pro-life movement, she got in touch with Sister Paula.

"She said I could help with the magazine that they were putting out," said Wensley. "I became one of the editors, creating little snippets of pro-life news." But she was soon to become Sister's travelling companion too.

"She found out about this international pro-life conference to be held in Ostend, Belgium, and she wanted to go so badly to hear Father Paul Marx," said Wensley. Father Marx was ordained a priest in 1947 in the order of St. Benedict and became an outspoken pro-life advocate, traveling around the world on behalf of the movement and writing books on the subject.

"Sister Paula couldn't go to the conference because all Sisters of Social Service had to have a companion on trips," explained Wensley. "So, I said, I'll go with you." The two women flew to Europe and attended the conference. Then they rented a car and drove around the country, toured the Rhine River and got completely lost trying to visit relatives of Sister Paula's who lived in Belgium. At one point they were about to rent a room in a hotel near a railway station when Wensley realized they were in a brothel—and hustled Sister Paula out as quickly as possible! They continued on to

London where Wensley's husband met them and then flew home.

"She was very intelligent," remembered Wensley. "She was persistent and had no qualms about asking anybody for anything because [the pro-life efforts] were so important. She never got upset—even with people who didn't like her—she loved them back. She was a positive person, always just full of creative ideas for a conference, or how to approach some piece of legislature, or for anything that came up."

Recalling Sister Paula's warm nature, Wensley said, "To know her was to love her."

Every year at Christmas, Sister Paula invited friends and colleagues to her Los Angeles apartment for food, music, and singing.

"Even though I was not in her group she used to invite me to her Christmas party," recalled Anne Hennessy. "She'd play the piano and we would sing Christmas songs and have gift exchanges people—it was hilarious. Christmas was obviously important to her. She asked everyone to do a talent show at the end."

And she made her Sisters laugh. Even in the darkest moments, she kept her faith and inspired others to keep working with optimism. And though she was fiercely dedicated to the cause which was inspired by God, she never spoke harshly to people who disagreed with her views on abortion.

This unique mix of willingness to tell the truth while being compassionate and kind made Sister Paula so remarkable.

"She was born a saint," said Betty Odello, RN, MN, retired professor of philosophy. She serves on the L.A. Archdiocese Life, Justice and Peace Commission, and worked with Sister Paula at the Scholl Institute as a speaker and writer about bioethics and end of life issues. "She understood the problems people experience. And she could speak at the conferences to volunteers, and also bring in excellent speakers too, and pull all these conversations together."

"She was an extremely strong, sweet, humble woman," said Nancy Corbett. Corbett remembered that for the first Christmas parties, Sister Paula's piano playing was not proficient but that did not stop her. "It was kind of rough in the beginning, but she was determined to keep going until she hit that right key," said Corbett.

When it came to money, Sister Paula was not afraid to ask for donations, but sometimes her colleagues in the business world had to push her to ask for more in fundraising.

"With donors, she laid out the needs and asked what they could do," remembered Odello. "Bob [Barbera] would say, 'You're not asking for more?' And then she would be shocked when they *would* give more."

Volunteers for Life

In 1997, in her continuing effort to inspire new leaders in the movement, Sister Paula invited college-age young women to get involved in a new program called Volunteers for Life.

"Through a federal government plan, graduating students owing a federal loan would be allowed to reduce the debt if the student volunteered at a non-profit," explained Robert Barbera. "Sister Paula asked me to form Volunteers for Life and become president. She prepared the necessary application to carry on the program. Over the next several years applicants were approved and performed volunteering services at different pro-life agencies."

At the time, Sister Paula wrote: "I really see the young people being very, very pro-life. It's apparent in the increase in statistics and apparent in the young people coming into the movement." And young women in the midst of a pregnancy crisis might more easily speak with counselors who were close in age. "[Clients] are not churched generally, but there's a spiritual sensitivity and they're coming in larger numbers to the centers," she said.

With the commitment of prayer and one year of work for the pro-life movement, these Volunteers for Life worked at counseling centers and other locations that were in need of extra staff—"wherever there is a pro-life need," explained Sister Paula at the time. They all lived in a Christ-centered community with a passionate shared purpose. "It was like AmeriCorps," remembered Mechtild Grothues.

Grothues explained that some students were finishing college, and some wanted to take a year off from college to work in fields that interested them. "In their hearts, these women already had a passion for pro-life work," she said. They went to Mass and shared the cooking and cleaning. It was like a little community. It was really unusual. They had to adhere to our standards. At least living chaste lives, and pro-life not for birth control."

Joseph Kay and his wife Pat were on the Board of Directors for Volunteers for Life and were moved by Sister Paula's work. "We revere the life and tireless effort of Sister Paula on behalf of the Pro-Life movement, as well as the great legacy she has left in her work with the Sisters of Social Service & International Life Services!" Kay wrote upon her death.

The unique gift that Sister Paula wanted to transmit to others was an understanding of how to sensitively help women who were pregnant and in crisis about their circumstances.

Beth Diemert, director of Affiliate Services for Heartbeat International, put it this way: "Her understanding of the need to create a relationship with the client and rely on the Holy Spirit to guide you in the interaction really struck home with me and affirmed my contributions at Heartbeat in the same way through the years."

Knowing that pro-life work would be necessary long after her death, Sister Paula was eager to prepare young people who would carry on after her.

Some pregnancy centers went a step further to become licensed clinics that could offer pregnancy tests and sonograms to pregnant women. Taking the legal and practical steps to become a clinic could take years, as numerous many regulations had to be followed precisely including exact dimensions of an examining room and the involvement of a doctor, a nurse, and a licensed sonographer. Many were willing to take those steps to be able to offer more services to women.

Bring It On!

Sister Paula was many things: Listener, advisor, counselor, fund-raiser, inspirational speaker. In fact, she lectured and conducted trainings in fifty states as well as in Australia, Ireland, Belgium, and Croatia.

And she was a fighter.

When confronted with laws that challenged pro-life work, her response was "Bring it on!"

Over the years, well-funded pro-life organizations wanted to absorb International Life Services, according to her friend Robert Barbera. "The problem was the executives from these agencies were compromised to water-down the pro-life movement. Sister Paula showed her strength of purity of purpose not to be comprised with watered down pro-life movement."

Then came a major showdown. In 2015 a law

proposed in California mandated that pro-life pregnancy counselling centers provide information about where and how to get an abortion to women who came for counseling.

Sister Paula, and all other pro-life advocates, were outraged that counsellors were going to be forced to go against their fundamental beliefs by giving out information about abortion.

She wrote this in the August 2016 newsletter for ILS:

> "The CA legislature passed a bill that tries to force our centers to give clients information where they can get an abortion. California also passed an assisted suicide bill this year. All of our centers have been experiencing what I call harassment inquiries from the CA State Department.
>
> "Centers have been accused of not turning in reports that were turned in. They have had to spend hours duplicating and explaining things. One of the California Centers, not an ILS Center, was denied their application for Clinic Status in spite of being cleared by NIFLA and seemingly all appropriate

steps were taken. "The Centers in Illinois are fighting an Illinois State bill that would force their Doctors to refer for abortion. But you know, it has not slowed us down. Mothers and babies are still coming in and receiving help. The enemy of our human nature is not winning. Bring it on. We are protected by prayer and we can handle these problems."

The National Institute of Family and Life Advocates, or NIFLA, led by Tom Glessner stepped up and filed a lawsuit in 2016 that challenged this law—the case eventually went all the way to the Supreme Court in 2018, and on June 26 of that year, the Supreme Court ruled in favor of the pro-life pregnancy centers.

Glessner, a lawyer and founder of NIFLA, invited Sister Paula to come to Washington and speak out against it. "She was kind and thoughtful, but she was tough, and she stood up for the movement," recalled Tom. "She told me later that it was the highlight in all her years of pro-life work to be able to speak a message of life in front of the Supreme Court steps."

In a recorded video made the year before she

died, Sister Paula described what happened at the steps of the Supreme Court the day the case was going to be heard, and the memory brought her to tears:

"It was pouring rain and freezing cold. When we got there, we found out there is no place to really gather for a rally, there was just a sidewalk in front of the Supreme Court and that's where rallies happen."

Pro-life groups were gathering—but so was a crowd with opposing views.

"The pro-life students in Washington, D.C. had stayed up all night long in the freezing rain and cold and slept on the sidewalk to save a place for us so we had a place in front of the Supreme Court. So, when we got there, it was all ready for us because of our pro-life young help. We set up our microphones and we had a number of great speakers from all over the United States"—and this included Sister Paula—"and our opponents set up next to us with a bunch of people and they had their speakers, and they made their speakers as loud as possible to drown out us. So, we had two speakers speaking at opposite ends of the spectrum! And of course, the media was there, and they were interviewing people. We just didn't pay attention, we kept speaking and it kept raining and it was cold and we were all freezing. We all just stayed there. Finally, at the end of about two hours of them trying to outshout us, all of a sudden, all the noise stopped. There was absolute utter silence. All you could hear was our speakers. What happened to them? They packed up their stuff and left. I asked—and found out that they were paid protesters. And when two hours had passed, they all left. Of course, our people were still standing there in the rain and cold until our lawyers came out and told us they had been heard. That was a big impression on me because I thought to myself, 'We're on the winning side. They're never going to win. Not as long as we're standing out in the rain and freezing cold, with our students standing out there all night long making a place for us. They have no chance of winning. We have the Holy Spirit with us.' That was a real lesson to me about the strength of the movement, and I have never forgotten it."

When laws, regulations or politicians challenged the workings of pregnancy counseling centers, Sister Paula's response was this: "You know, it has not slowed us down. Mothers and babies are still coming in and receiving help. The enemy of our human nature is not winning. Bring it on. We are protected by prayer and we can handle these problems."

By staying the course, and guided by the Holy Spirit, the movement would prevail. This powerful sense of purpose and willingness to persist is one of the great reasons why Sister Paula's work was successful.

"Sister Paula was tempted to have an easy time more than once," remembered Robert Barbera. "At one interview with a wealthy group, they said they would support her if she would compromise on the exact time when life begins. Sister Paula resisted the temptation and was courageous—and did not get their support. Several other groups also asked for compromise and she resisted."

Hope After Abortion

SOME WOMEN DO CHOOSE ABORTION. SISTER PAULA of course knew this—and one measure of her compassion was her understanding that women who chose abortion sometimes suffered terribly for years after. Instead of judging or condemning them, she felt they should be forgiven, loved and reconciled with God.

After Sister Paula's death one woman wrote lovingly about the help she received from Sister Paula after her abortion—the pregnancy was the result of rape and Sister Paula helped her to heal.

Sister Paula gave support to Project Rachel, an outreach from the Catholic Church which seeks to help women who've had an abortion recover emotionally and spiritually. She wrote: "The Church is a place of healing. It speaks the truth about abortion to men and women contemplating this action. 'Don't do it! It is wrong and it will hurt you and the baby,' but it also speaks the full truth: 'If you have had an abortion, God's mercy is great enough to forgive that, too.' Jesus offers forgiveness and healing. He offers the hope and promise of resurrection and reunion with the child who is waiting for his parents in heaven."

Donna Sorek remembers many women who would seek out help from her Ventura County Center. "So many clients would come back, and this is why Sister Paula encouraged us to learn to deal with post-abortion loss. She knew about this and I saw it in clients, over and over. Clients would come in after they'd had an abortion. It is common among women who've had an abortion to get birthday candles for the date her child would have been born—they also find themselves pregnant again. They had a deep-seated need to replace the baby they had lost. Every abortion has its own story. Every client has her own story."

Anne Hennessy, former Executive Director of the Right to Life League of Southern California, put it this way: "It's not something that goes away for many people. It stays and festers and people have differing levels of problems, from a slight disturbance or depression up to and including suicide. It's a problem that affects many people. But they go through the healing process, and heal their relationship with their God, this can ripple out." Hennessy met Sister Paula around 2007 and was impressed by her post abortion counselling. "I hired Sister to do several trainings over the years, mostly to women where were counselling in hope and healing after abortion."

She recalled that when Sister Paula met with women who sought counseling after having an abortion, she would ask them to write a letter to the baby and name the baby. Over a number of sessions, she would encourage the women to hold a little memorial for the baby and work to restore a relationship to God. "There were women who had really serious issues that regular lay counselors can't help so they would be referred to therapists," said Hennessey. "A lot of women who go to pregnancy help centers are healing after an abortion. Often some of those counselors have gone through an abortion themselves, so they understand."

Women who would choose abortion were never turned away. "They are always invited back to the clinic and accepted with love and a caring and listening ear," said Hennessey.

Sister Paula's extraordinary sensitivity and understanding of women who've had an abortion is obvious in her writings:

> "Society tells young women that abortion will solve their problem. It says nothing about the problems abortion creates. Supporters of abortion claim it is a simple procedure with no lasting impact. And women who know better don't discuss, certainly not publicly, how abortion changed their lives for the worse.
>
> "Abortion is an extremely unnatural experience for a woman's body and her maternal instinct. But if society denies the mother's loss, her body does not. God prepares a woman psychologically and physically for motherhood. When a woman is pregnant she feels different. Within a few days after conception, even before the tiny embryo has nested in her uterine wall, a hormone called 'early pregnancy factor' is found in her bloodstream, alerting the cells of her body to the pregnancy. Her body may now crave different foods, she may need

more rest. New cells begin to grow in her breasts, cells which will mature and secrete milk specially formulated for the needs of a newborn. She begins to think 'baby.' She starts noticing babies on the street, in the store, on television. She may dream about her baby at night and fantasize about her baby during the day. What name? Who will he or she look like?

"But if she wants to have an abortion she must try to stop this process. She must deny the maternal feelings entering into her consciousness. She must believe that what is inside of her is not fully a baby. She must stop the process of thinking about her baby as 'her baby.'

"Negative reactions are to be expected and do not depend on a person's religious beliefs or general mental health. Although her mind may say one thing, her emotional life and her body cells say another. If she has the abortion, the very cells of her body remember the pregnancy and know that the process of change that had been going on was stopped in an unnatural manner. Her body and her emotions tell her that she is a mother who has lost a child. And so it is not surprising that after the abortion, a pain begins to emerge from the depths of her heart. She has a loss to mourn but cannot allow herself to grieve. Grieving would require admitting to herself that a child was killed in the abortion and that she shares responsibility for her child's death. This is a very heavy burden to bear.

"Women, and all those involved in the decision to abort, must believe, or try to believe, that there was no human life present in the womb. To admit this is to admit complicity in the killing of an innocent human being. Condemning abortion would mean condemning themselves or the wife, daughter, sister or friend whom they love. And so society refuses to recognize the incontrovertible facts about human life before birth.

"Everyone is a part of the healing ministry of Christ. A simple word that will touch their hearts and release them from fear and isolation can begin the healing process. While law and society often pit the interests of a mother against those of her unborn child, the Church recognizes that their best interests are joined. What is best for the child is also best for the mother. We need to speak the full truth: 'If you have had an abortion, God's mercy is great enough to forgive that, too.' Jesus offers forgiveness and healing. You will come to understand that nothing is definitively lost and you will also be able to ask forgiveness from your child, who is now living in the Lord. Jesus offers the hope and promise of resurrection and reunion with the child who is waiting for his parents in heaven."

End-of-Life Issues

RESPECTING THE SANCTITY OF LIFE MEANS ALL LIFE, from beginning to end.

Sister Paula was concerned about end-of-life issues related to physician-assisted suicide, and removal of life support, as well as bioengineering issues such as cloning. And she believed that an educated public was crucial to making wise decisions—including which laws to enact. This led Sister Paula to establish the Scholl Institute in the early 1980s, a Judeo-Christian nonprofit that brought together professionals in medicine, law, psychology, and religion with the goal of educating the public.

Sister Paula invited some of her close pro-life allies to join the Scholl Institute. She asked Betty Odello, a nurse and professor of bioethics, to work with her—and Odello was soon appointed president. "We did a lot of speaking together," recalled Odello, who'd started a bioethics program at Pierce College. "The International Life Services worked on beginning of life issues. We at Scholl Institute were interested in dignity of the human being at the end of life."

A speakers bureau was created so that the Scholl Institute could send professional experts to give talks to organizations about these topics, and printed materials were produced for interested individuals and groups.

Odello did not believe these issues were necessarily based in religion and was happy to speak to atheist societies as well as church parishes. She and Sister Paula were often challenged by people who did not agree with their views—but in these encounters, Sister Paula always remained calm. "When it came to talking to people, Sister Paula was second to none," Odello said. If someone in an audience posed a challenging question, she would gently restate the question in such a way that disarmed the challenger. "She never seemed to get riled," recalled Odello. "She always answered lovingly. I don't know where she got her patience. People would come to our lectures who were really interested in what we had to say."

Sister Paula was never tempted to argue, belittle or silence people who disagreed with her. "Sister Paula was just such a positive person," said Odello. "She was the closest thing to a saint I'll ever meet. She was always thinking of other people and always so positive."

In defending issues related to the end of life, Sister Paula was willing to travel to Sacramento and Washington to protest or advocate her position to legislators directly.

"Sister Paula expanded International Life Services by producing material to halt assisted suicide," recalled Robert Barbera. "At the time the issue was gaining popularity because some states in the U.S. were legalizing euthanasia. Sister Paula had an attorney who worked on his own time to write a bill to not allow the legalization of euthanasia. The bill and was turned over to a sponsoring assemblyman. It was necessary to lobby on behalf of the bill and to give testimony. Sister Paula arranged for myself, the attorney, a doctor, and a woman who been comatose for a year and then woke up, to appear before the California State Assembly," Barbera recalled.

"We drove up to Sacramento the day before and slept at a large dormitory occupied by a

Catholic order to be fresh for the next day to testify on behalf of the bill. The attorney and doctor each gave a great presentation. The lady who had been in a coma and had come back to life shocked the assembly and it seemed the bill would go through. But we had a surprise adversary who spoke. The assembly took a break and ended without voting, thus ending the bill," Barbera explained. "Ultimately, we did not win that cause, but I'm sure we had an impact."

Sister Paula's Legacy

Sister Paula never wanted to draw attention to herself. She believed that her work was God's work, powered by the Holy Spirit. In fact, she probably would not have wanted this book to be written. She saved many lives and inspired many people to carry on the pro-life work for the generations after her.

In her lifetime she received many awards, including the United States Conference of Catholic Bishops' People of Life Award for lifetime commitment to the pro-life movement and the Lagatus Cardinal John O'Connor Pro-Life Award. This book aims to keep alive the spirit of Sister Paula so that her work is recognized and continues.

Many people never knew that Sister Paula had diabetes from an early age because she never let it slow her down or get in the way of her activities. In her later years she developed additional health problems including cancer and heart trouble.

"All through the years of Sister Paula's life she was sick and often hospitalized nearing death," recalled Robert Barbera. "She would recover and go home again, revitalized to carry on her mission. She never talked about her illness and only cared about others. Along with the pro-life issue she embraced the down-and-out marginalized people in the neighborhood."

In her final days family and friends visited Sister Paula, some of whom still remember vividly her last words.

"She said, 'Pray that it's soon,'" remembered Nancy Corbett the former executive director of the Mission Hills Pregnancy Counseling Center. "She said it with a smile— 'Just pray that's soon.' It stuck with me. I thought: She's ready. She's at peace and ready."

Dennis Di Pietro saw Sister Paula three days before she died. "She sounded weak, but her words were the same and she smiled a lot," he remembered.

Daniel Mansueto, president of ILS, talked to

Sister Paula in the months before her death about her health, and suggested various treatments. "She was very interested, she did not want to die," he recalled. "She said 'If there is one in a hundred chance of success, I want it!'" But her condition got worse and worse, and Mansueto visited her as she lay on her death bed. "She was very obviously dying," he remembered. "I said, you know you're dying. She said, 'I accept that and I'm ready to die.' The thing of it was she was still happy. She still had all of her joy in her even in her dying."

"In the month preceding Sister Paula's death, she was relaxed and felt her prayers were answered," recalled Robert Barbera. "She touched the lives of so many people to make the choice not to abort to save lives."

Sister Paula died at age eighty-two in Glassell Park, Los Angeles, on August 13, 2021, surrounded by her closest companions and friends. Messages of love for her poured in from many corners of the world. Her loss was—and is still—mourned. But the dark-eyed nun from Kansas City left many inspired colleagues and strong institutions that will continue the work she began.

"She made the world a better place by showing

us, through her own life, how joyful and beautiful life can be when lived in service to God and others," Mansueto stated.

Sainthood

"She was born a saint."
—*Betty Odello, Scholl Institute*

It's difficult to measure the impact that Sister Paula had on people who knew her or to count the lives she saved. The numbers are great.

As Betty Odello's words indicate, Sister Paula had a unique presence that could move and transform those around her. Many people use the word "saint" in trying to describe her. Around Sister Paula, anger would turn to compassion, inertia would turn to action, discouragement would turn to joy.

"My years with Sister Paula gave me purpose to defend lives," said Robert Barbera. "Now that she passed away, I have my regrets. She persevered in the movement and never compromised on the practical solution. In my last visit to her a month before she died, I am reminded of all the good in life she represented. Her loyalty to the cause and not sacrificing integrity was important. Now that she is gone, I can still see the love in her eyes and in her smile. I can still remember her calling my name, Bob.

"My conscience is bursting with regrets that I did not do enough. Her life showed purpose now I want her death to show purpose. By creating the Society for Sister Paula—and pursing sainthood for her—I envision Sister Paula as a poster person for the pro-life movement. Recognizing her for beatification will elevate the pro-life cause and give her the recognition she so well deserves. This Society recognizes hearts have to be won not through the legal system but through compassion."

Who are saints and why are they singled out among all others?

Many people who knew Sister Paula believe she certainly qualifies as a saint. She was a blessing to whoever she met—she was kind, generous and sympathetic. She spent her entire adult life being God's messenger to save life. Is this not the work of a saint? If so, then proposing her for official beatification makes sense.

The beatification for Sister Paula by the Church is a tremendous undertaking. According to the U.S. Conference of Catholic Bishops, there are three steps to sainthood: A candidate becomes "venerable," then "blessed," then "saint," with certain requirements of the candidate's life at each stage, including miracles taking place through the candidate's intersession.

"Sister Paula's history speaks for itself," said Barbera. "Her dedication to save lives through her life's work was significant and noble. It is important to recognize Sister Paula to put an image for volunteers to continue their pro-life cause to rally upon. That she did not want to be recognized was a testament to her humility. Her life's work was no ordinary life by an ordinary person but by a special person."

In a tribute to Sister Paula, the president of International Life Services Daniel Mansueto wrote this:

"Sister Paula's pro-life resume, as impressive as it is, does not begin to capture what she brought to the pro-life movement. In a unique way Sister

Paula radiated the joy and love that animate the pro-life movement. She was genuinely a gift of God to us and our cause. May God reward her for all her holy service to the pro-life movement and bless her soul forever."

Afterword

The Divine Grace of God
by Robert Barbera

(Excerpted from the forthcoming book,
American Exceptionalism.*)*

The question of abortion is arguably the most contentious issue of our time—correction, of *all* time—as well as the most complex. It divides families and polarizes the religious and the secular, Republicans and Democrats, young and old, men and women. More single-issue voters cast their ballots based on a candidate's position on abortion and government funding of clinics such as Planned Parenthood than on health care, immigration, economic policy, or gun control.

I am a Catholic. I believe that all life comes from the divine grace of God. But I know that not everyone shares my faith or beliefs. Turning abortion into a fight between believers and non-believers or a conflict between church and state only muddies the waters. If you don't believe in the same god as I do, or any god at all, I'm not going to be able to use religious morality to convince you that abortion is wrong. When the religious use doctrine to argue their position on abortion with non-believers, they've already lost the argument.

The decisions we make in life—no matter how big or small—are based on a combination of the sympathetic/emotional and logical/analytical options that come from our hearts and our brains. When discussing abortion, those on both sides are often driven by their hearts and when it comes to using their brains, select only the facts that support and validate their feelings. While we need to listen to the compassionate callings from our hearts, decisions based purely on our feelings are rarely sound. To understand those who differ with us—especially on an issue that inspires such passion—we must temper our hearts and heed the information and objective findings of science. So, please bear with me and keep an open mind while

I push my religion and my passion about the issue aside and focus on facts and logic.

At the most basic level, abortion comes down to two questions: When does life begin? And does one person have the right to take another's life? With the exception of the evil among us, we can all answer the latter question with an unequivocal "no." The answer to the former question has been a little murkier.

Until the Age of Enlightenment and the invention of the microscope in the 17th century, a prevalent theory about procreation was that each human being comes from a series of nesting dolls—dormant inside either a man or a woman. People had a *general* idea of how babies were made, but absolutely no understanding of the science involved. It's easy to laugh at our ill-informed ancestors and we can forgive them their ignorance and confusion as to when life begins. They couldn't possibly know better. But, we do. Yet, despite all the objective scientific evidence available to us today, we still can't agree on when life begins.

When does life begin?

The *entire* pro-choice argument rests on the

position that if an unborn baby is not a human being, then how can killing it be a crime? So, we get trapped in discussions about when is a life a life and a baby a baby and when does life begin. This debate may have had its place fifty or more years ago, but to presume to ask such questions now is utterly disingenuous.

Some believe that life begins at insemination. Starting in preschool, our children are taught that a baby is made when a sperm inseminates an egg.

But most adults don't know that at that moment, the *entirety* of that new human being's DNA is complete. Think about how much we love DNA—whether to solve decades' old cold cases or learn about our heritage through mail order kits. All of that genetic information is held in the zygote before it even travels to the uterus. Who knows, with advances in the sciences, it's possible that a 3D virtual rendering could be made of that human being at any age. I wonder if we could "see" the potential of those unborn babies, would people feel differently about never giving them an opportunity to live.

We can all agree that life ends when the heart stops beating. It makes sense then that the reverse would be true—that life begins when the heart *starts* beating. But this simple logic is inconvenient for those who argue in favor of abortion. With current technology an unborn child's heartbeat can be heard at eight weeks. Yet we know the heart actually begins to beat *just eighteen days after conception*— a far cry short of the twenty-four to twenty-six weeks that most US states permit abortions to be performed.

Just eight weeks after conception, another one of our unique identifiers begins to form—fingerprints. It's around this time that a baby exhibits reflex movement during invasive procedures. Have you seen the real-time ultrasound of the twelve-week-old unborn baby being aborted? I have, and I never want to see it again. It's absolutely chilling and certainly not for the faint-hearted. I dare you to watch it and tell me that the fetus—or *tissue* as some would call it—instinctively moving away from the abortionist's probing suction instrument as its heart rate elevates from 140 to 200 beats per minute, is not *alive*, not a *human being*, not a *baby*.

To me, the most egregious position assumed by the pro-abortion side is that of *viability*—that life begins when the unborn baby can survive outside the womb. It's like a young child who covers his own eyes and since he can't see you, believes you can't see him. Can anyone with any sense honestly believe that a baby only becomes a baby after it passes through the birth canal? And before that it's just tissue or a clump of cells? Almost as if a magical transformation happens in the moment of childbirth.

What's "viable" today wouldn't have been viable centuries—or even decades—ago. Scientific advances continue to move the bar. While a full-term pregnancy is forty weeks long, the most premature baby known to survive was born at an astonishing twenty-one weeks. At this printing a twenty-four-week-old baby has a 40 to 70% chance of survival outside the womb, yet most US states permit abortions to be performed up to twenty-two to twenty-four weeks.

What do you think? Does life begin at:

- conception when a person's DNA is formed
- eighteen days when the heart starts beating
- eight weeks when we can hear the heartbeat (with current technology)
- twenty-one weeks, when we know a baby can survive outside the womb (with current technology)

- twenty-four to twenty-six weeks (most US states at this publication date)

Whatever your answer, when would *you* be comfortable ending that life?

Hiding behind terminology

I know plenty of good, decent people who believe aborting a baby is okay. I think this is due to ignorance, in part because of the deliberate terminology abortion—excuse me, "pro-choice"—advocates use to distract and obfuscate.

Because the process of aborting a baby is so truly ghoulish, its supporters are encouraged to only use carefully chosen words and euphemisms. These phrases have become so commonplace and part of our vernacular that we don't even think about them anymore. Abortion proponents refer to unborn babies as *clumps of cells, fetal tissue, products of conception, part of the mother*, and worst of all, *medical waste*. Sayings such as *a woman's right to choose, reproductive freedom*, and *my body, my choice* serve to take the focus off the unseen baby and onto the "victimized" woman who we can see with our own eyes.

I can remember a time when an unborn baby was called a *baby*—not a *fetus*. It is no accident that it and terms like *extraction, induced miscarriage*, and *termination* are now part of our accepted nomenclature. Headlines don't read, "Man Aborts Wife After Argument" or "Truck Terminates Child Crossing Street." When discussing a serious illness, doctors talk about survival rates, not a person's *viability*. Rotten teeth are *extracted*.

I wonder how differently people would feel if we substituted expressions like

"terminating a pregnancy" and "extracting tissue from a woman's body" with "killing a baby" and "murdering the child inside a mother's womb."

What do you really know about abortion?

Our newspapers publish photographs of immigration detention centers, the homeless, and victims of war and poverty. These images often appeal to our emotions and our humanity and influence our opinions. It is important that we don't hide from injustices and the things that should, and do, upset us on a profound level. We have a responsibility to our fellow man to understand the suffering and pain in our world—especially on social issues on which we take a stance. Yet the entire business of abortion is shrouded from public view. As I just mentioned, this is the intention of its advocates and clinicians. But we are complicit too by turning a blind eye to what is really happening.

I challenge you to look on the internet and see for yourself what a sixteen-week-old unborn baby looks like. It doesn't look like a clump of tissue. It looks exactly like what it is—*a baby*. Its arms and legs are formed and able to move. Toenails, eyebrows and eyelashes can be seen, and it may even be possible to determine the baby's gender. Internally, all the major organs are formed. Though its eyes are still closed, they perceive light. Some have already begun to suck their thumbs. And they may be able to hear. Protected in the amniotic sac, the baby depends on a life-support system delivered from the placenta through the umbilical cord. But hardly so for the baby who is only doing exactly what nature has meant for it to do—living on a literal lifeline, presumably safe and sheltered from the outside world.

Most states permit abortions to be performed well beyond this stage of development and through the second semester. That's up to five or six months. Have you seen a five- to six-months pregnant woman and ever questioned that she was indeed carrying a new life?

Planned Parenthood describes the process of abortion as gentle. It may be for the mother who has been given numbing agents to help with the pain. I challenge you to watch the 1994 documentary, *The Silent Scream,* which shows real-time ultrasound imaging of a twelve-week-old baby being aborted. As the baby's heartrate elevates it is chilling to see the tiny being recoil in vain from the abortionist's tool.

While early-term abortions are performed by a suction device, a sixteen- to twenty-four-week-old week baby is simply too large to simply vacuum out of the womb. In *dilation and evacuation*, the abortionist must first use forceps to crush the baby's head before dismembering the body so it can be removed in pieces. Yes, I said *in pieces.* Sometimes they inject the baby's heart first with digoxin or potassium chloride to make sure it's indeed dead before its skull is crushed. This is considered a humane act.

Perhaps nothing is more grotesque than *dilation and extraction*, more familiarly known as "partial birth abortion." The "partial birth" part means that the baby is partially delivered—completely alive and feet first. At this point, the baby could be pulled out of the birth canal and cared for by doctors and nurses to ensure its survival. Instead, while half in and half out of its mother, the abortionist drills a hole at the base of its skull with a scissors so the baby's brain can be sucked out through a tube. At this point, the baby's skull collapses, making it small enough to be removed.

It is incumbent that every proponent of a "woman's right to choose" understands what they're really advocating.

What about unwanted pregnancies?

Unwanted pregnancies are a sad reality. And I ache for women and of course, girls, who find themselves in this position through no fault of their own from rape or incest. The men who inflict this violence are monsters. Victims of rape and incest bear the scars from their ordeals for the rest of their lives. Pro-choice advocates argue that it adds further trauma for their victims to carry these children for nine months and give birth. Yet this undermines the guilt and remorse many (unfortunately, not all) women feel after aborting their babies. When seeing the pregnancy through, some good comes from the crime against the mother—a new life that may improve her life in unexpected ways or bring joy to a childless couple.

To invoke a trite saying, "two wrongs don't make a right." Aborting a child conceived under such horrific circumstances doesn't undo any of the injustice a woman has suffered. Where there was one defenseless victim, there are now two. How can taking any life be considered a good thing or that it should be another person's decision? Pro-choicers imply that getting an abortion is a quick and easy procedure. In and out. Over and done. Out of sight, out of mind. Plenty of women who've had abortions would say otherwise and mourn their unborn children. Maybe bringing a new life into the world and either choosing to raise it or offering it to loving parents desperate for a child of their own can be a healing experience. And to that point, we need to make the adoption process easier and less bureaucratic.

I'm against capital punishment, but don't you find it an injustice that the criminal who created the life gets to keep his while his child's life is snuffed out? And what of children conceived in a consensual relationship? Should the father not have a say in what happens to his child? What about a man's right to choose?

What is the government's role?

A functional society depends on law and order. This includes the protection of its citizens' lives and punishment for those who take a life unlawfully. A moral society values and protects its weakest members. This includes the young, the elderly, and the mentally and physically infirm. It is our responsibility to defend those who can't defend themselves regardless of their perceived value to society.

I value life. I'm against abortion. I'm against capital punishment. To be human is to be flawed. How can any one of us have the audacity to presume that we know best if, when, how, or why another should die? Considering the many earlier examples of government inefficiency and mismanagement discussed in this book, how could we possibly entrust our elected officials with such monumental moral responsibility? We can't.

Maybe you don't agree with me or not on the ethics and legality of abortion, but I hope we can see eye-to-eye on the government's fiscal role.

The ease of availability has led to abortion-on-demand and too easy an out for couples who choose not to use birth control. Pro-choicers are trying to overturn the Hyde Amendment which prohibits federal Medicaid from funding abortions. That aside, seventeen states already use public funds to pay for abortions. According to the Guttmacher Institute, the state of California funded 88,466 abortions . . . in just 2014. I don't know about you, but that is certainly not how I want my tax dollars used.

Most abortions are performed at women's health clinics. The most well known is Planned Parenthood which receives over one-third of its annual revenue (over $1 billion) from government grants and contracts. Though the Hyde Amendment prohibits the government for giving Planned Parenthood money for abortions, giving the agency over $500 million for the other health services and contraception it provides makes it possible for it to devote the rest of its budget to providing abortions. Without these fungible government funds, Planned Parenthood couldn't afford to continue with abortions which helps explain their $6.5 million contribution to candidates and political parties in 2014.

Given the sorry state of our politicians' fiscal

spending and considering our shortcomings in educating our children, taking care of our veterans, and our decrepit infrastructure, how can we possibly justify diverting funds that would enrich our nation's future citizens to finance something that is morally corrupt, largely preventable and, for the most part, determined by individual citizen's choices?

Unwanted pregnancies happen. They have since the beginning of time and that's not going to change. They are an unfortunate fact of life and something with which individuals, families, and cultures must contend.

As caring people, we should continue to do everything we can to minimize unwanted pregnancies and at the same time, make the adoption process easier for all involved.

Sister Paula Vandegaer, 2020

Sources

In addition to interviews with numerous friends and colleagues about Sister Paula, the following resources were used:

The New York Times February 8, 1976 "Reagan Affirms Anti-Abortion Stand" https://www.nytimes.com/1976/02/08/archives/reagan-affirms-antiabortion-stand.html

National Review January 22, 2008 "Reagan's Darkest Hour" https://www.nationalreview.com/2008/01/reagans-darkest-hour-paul-kengor-patricia-clark-doerner/

Foot Soldiers Armed with Love: Heartbeat International's First Forty Years by Margaret H. (Peggy) Hartshorn, Ph.D. Copyright 2014 by Margaret H. (Peggy) Hartshorn, Ph.D.

Introduction to Pregnancy Counseling by Sister Paula Vandegaer, L.C.S.W. Copyright 1999 by

International Life Services; Los Angeles, California

California Association of Natural Family Planning May 27, 2017 "Questioning, Accepting, Believing" by Sister Paula Vandegaer
https://www.canfp.org/newsletter/6867/

International Life Services website
https://www.internationallifeservices.org/
Tribute to Sister Paula by Daniel Mansueto
Los Angeles Catholic Angelus September 15, 2021 "Friends, advocates mourn passing of California's pro-life 'godmother'"
https://angelusnews.com/local/la-catholics/friends-advocates-mourn-passing-of-californias-pro-life-godmother/

Heartbeat International "The Ground is Tilled and the Seed is Planted by the "Greatest Generation""
https://www.heartbeatinternational.org/heartbeat-history

United States Conference of Catholic Bishops "After the Abortion" by Sister Paula

Vandegaer 1999" https://www.usccb.org/committees/pro-life-activities/after-abortion-sister-paula-vandegaer-1999

La Habra Life Newsletter Winter/Spring 2016 http://uploads.weconnect.com/mce/4707f92226a773ddf1b2602948b881004c8a96e9/Whats%20New/Whats%20New%202016/WinterSpring2016Newslett%20erditedEmaili.pdf

Volunteers for Life: From the California Catholic Conference, November 2011 https://www.volunteersforlife.com/our-founder-sr-paula.html

Pregnancy Help News August 19, 2021 "Heartbeat International co-founder, pioneer in the pregnancy help movement, dies" https://pregnancyhelpnews.com/heartbeat-international-co-founder-pioneer-in-the-pregnancy-help-movement-dies

www.ingramcontent.com/pod-product-compliance
Lightning Source LLC
Chambersburg PA
CBHW022009120526
44592CB00034B/755